The Wealth Manifestation Code: Clearing 33 Energy Blocks to Unlock Abundance

Simon Bedros

THE WEALTH MANIFESTATION CODE

Copyright © 2023 by Simon Bedros

Third Edition Released 2026

All rights reserved. No part of this book may be reproduced, stored in a retrieval system, or transmitted in any form or by any means, electronic, mechanical, photocopying, recording, or otherwise, without written permission from the author.

Disclaimer:

"The Wealth Manifestation Code: Clearing 33 Energy Blocks to Unlock Abundance" is based on the author's personal knowledge, insights and experiences. While it aims to positively influence and inspire, it cannot and does not guarantee financial or material wealth.

The effectiveness of its teachings varies per individual, and applying the principles is a personal choice. Responsibility for any decisions and their consequences rests with the reader.

Opening words by the author:

Your path to abundance is unique.
Walk it with an open heart, a clear mind, and the courage to embrace change.

THE WEALTH MANIFESTATION CODE

Table of Contents

Preface

Introduction

Part I: Understanding the Wealth Manifestation Code

Chapter 1: The Law of Attraction and Wealth Manifestation

Chapter 2: The 33 Energy Blocks to Manifesting Wealth

Part II: Clearing Energy Blocks with the Wealth Manifestation Code

Chapter 3: Clearing Energy Blocks Related to Money Mindset

Chapter 4: Clearing Energy Blocks Related to Self-Worth and Self-Value

Chapter 5: Clearing Energy Blocks Related to Relationships and Social Conditioning

Chapter 6: Applying the Wealth Manifestation Code Techniques

Part III: Integrating the Wealth Manifestation Code into Your Life

Chapter 7: Building a Wealth Manifestation Mindset

Chapter 8: Taking Action with the Wealth Manifestation Code

Conclusion

The Power Phrases

Frequently Asked Questions

About the Author

Preface

Hey you, beloved individual,

Although I may not know you personally, the fact that you've landed on this book means that our paths are aligned. The Higher Power of this Universe—whether you call it God, Allah, HA-SHEM, Infinite Intelligence, Source, or the Universe—has led you to this book for a reason. You are here because you have an intention for a better, more joyful, and prosperous future, and I'm delighted to be your guide on this personal journey through this book.

It has been some time since I released the last edition of this book. Since then, I have refined, improved, and strengthened many of the methods and teachings within it.

This was not because the original teachings were incomplete, but because the feedback and questions I received helped me sharpen and deepen what was already there.

If you are holding this latest edition, you are truly fortunate, because you are receiving the very best of this material. Much of what is now in your hands was once shared only with members of my inner circle program and long-term students.

Now, I have chosen to make more of it available to you so that more people can benefit from it. I believe the time has come for more people to access these teachings and begin manifesting the lives they truly desire.

Welcome to *The Wealth Manifestation Code: Clearing 33 Energy Blocks to Unlock Abundance*. This book is born from my personal journey of transformation and the desire to share the powerful techniques that have helped me and countless others unlock a life of abundance. It has been distributed and purchased by people from all around the world, influencing lives globally.

Some of the teachings in this book may seem familiar, especially if you've read Rhonda Byrne's transformative work, *The Secret*. While *The Secret* is an excellent book, and I commend Rhonda for bringing it to the world, it leaves out a crucial element in manifestation: energy blocks and the importance of clearing them.

THE WEALTH MANIFESTATION CODE

Everything around you is composed of energy, and the energy you radiate is what you attract back to you. Many who read *The Secret*, no matter how hard they work and try, struggle to manifest their desires because they have energetic blocks in their field. This deeper approach to clearing these blocks has led many to call this book *The Secret 2.0* or even *The Secret of The Secret*.

Through this guide, I aim to help you clear these blocks and achieve the life you dream of and desire. This book is not a book to read just once and forget about; it is a book you will <u>read over and over again</u>, ensuring you apply the teachings. Through constant evaluation and application, you can make sure you are well on your way to abundance.

As you read this book, you will notice that certain quotes and phrases are repeated throughout. This is intentional, because repetition works. These are power phrases designed to sink deeper into your mind, **help activate** *The Wealth Manifestation Code* within you, and clear the energy blocks that may be standing in the way of the abundance and wealth you desire.

After finishing the book, I highly suggest you read the *Frequently Asked Questions* section, as it includes additional valuable information you will not want to miss. I look forward to hearing about the positive transformations you will experience as a result of applying this material.

With much love,

Simon Bedros

Introduction

Are you ready to unlock your potential for abundance and financial freedom? If you have been trapped in a cycle of scarcity, struggling to make ends meet, or working tirelessly without seeing the results you desire, then *The Wealth Manifestation Code* may be the beginning of a profound transformation.

This book is designed to guide you toward greater wealth and abundance by helping you identify and clear the energy blocks that may be holding you back. In doing so, it opens the way for you to begin creating the financial future you have long desired.

What sets this book apart from other financial self-help guides is its holistic approach and the deeper insight it offers—an insight that, while not entirely hidden, has often been overlooked in mainstream discussions. The focus on 33 energy blocks is directly linked to the 33 vertebrae in the human spine. In ancient mystery schools and esoteric traditions, the spine was often regarded as more than a physical structure. It was seen as an important channel or transmitter of energy, intimately connected to the flow of life within us.

From this perspective, when that inner channel is burdened, blocked, or out of alignment, a person may feel hindered in the ability to manifest the life they desire. That is, in many ways, what these energy blocks do. They interfere with your natural flow. They weigh down your vision, your confidence, your emotional clarity, and your ability to move forward with strength and purpose.

Think of the human spine as a kind of inner staff. Symbolically, it is your support, your strength, and your channel. Just as Moses' staff was an instrument of power, your own "staff" must be functioning well if you are to move through life with alignment, force, and purpose. If the staff is hindered, it cannot part the Red Sea. In much the same way, if you are struggling to manifest the life you desire, it may be a sign that something within you is blocked, burdened, or not working as it should.

And while there are certainly exceptions, it is not hard to notice that many people living unhappy, burdened lives also carry chronic tension or ongoing issues in the spine, as though the weight within eventually begins to show itself physically as well.

At times, this can feel like trying to climb a mountain while carrying a massive rock on your back. Even if you cannot see the weight, you can feel it. You feel the heaviness. You feel the resistance. You feel that something is making the journey harder than it should be.

And that matters, because not everything real is visible to the eye. What we humans can see with our physical eyes is only 0.0035% of the entire electromagnetic spectrum—less than 1%—called visible light. Much of what shapes our lives is unseen, yet deeply felt. As Neville Goddard said, "Feeling is the secret." If you can feel the burden, then the burden is real in its effects, whether you can see it or not.

The Wealth Manifestation Code sheds light on this often-overlooked wisdom, guiding you through each of the 33 energy blocks that may be hindering your financial success. Throughout these pages, you will learn how to develop a wealth mindset, create a financial plan that aligns with your values and goals, and use powerful techniques such as meditation, visualization, affirmations, and energy healing to clear the blocks that may be limiting your progress.

So, are you ready to unlock *The Wealth Manifestation Code* and begin manifesting the abundance you deserve? Let us embark on this enlightening journey together and open the path to greater freedom, prosperity, and fulfillment.

Part I:
Understanding the Wealth Manifestation Code

Chapter 1:
The Law of Attraction and Wealth Manifestation

"Believe and you shall receive. Doubt and you shall go without."

Do you believe that the universe has the power to bring abundance into your life? If so, then you're already familiar with the Law of Attraction. The Law of Attraction is the belief that we attract into our lives whatever we focus on, whether positive or negative. In other words, what we think about and feel, we bring about.

On a fundamental level, you attract what you are in the present moment—what you are vibrationally aligned with through the thoughts, feelings, and emotional state you consistently radiate.

When it comes to manifesting wealth, the Law of Attraction can play a powerful role. By aligning your thoughts and emotions with abundance, you can attract opportunities, resources, and abundance into your life. This can include anything from financial abundance to opportunities for career advancement, to deep and meaningful relationships.

However, the Law of Attraction is not a magic formula. It requires more than just positive thinking and visualization. You must also take action towards your goals, and make conscious choices that align with your desires. In addition, the Law of Attraction is often hindered by negative thought patterns and limiting beliefs that can create energy blocks.

So, what are energy blocks? Energy blocks are negative thought patterns, limiting beliefs, emotional burdens, and other barriers that prevent you from creating the life you desire. These blocks can stem from a variety of sources, including ancestral patterns or family beliefs, societal conditioning, past traumas, and personal insecurities. They can manifest in the form of self-doubt, fear of failure, scarcity mindset, and other mental and emotional barriers that hold you back from achieving your full potential.

But by clearing these blocks, you can open yourself up to the abundance that the universe has to offer. This is where *The Wealth Manifestation Code* comes in. This book takes a holistic approach to wealth creation by addressing the underlying energy blocks that can hold you back from manifesting abundance.

By combining practical strategies with powerful techniques such as meditation, visualization, and energy healing, you can clear these blocks and unlock your potential for wealth and financial freedom. *The Wealth Manifestation Code* is designed to help you achieve success in all areas of your life, from your career to your relationships to your finances.

In this chapter, we'll explore the role of the Law of Attraction in wealth manifestation and how it can help you create the life you desire. We'll also delve into the energy blocks that can prevent you from fully harnessing the power of the Law of Attraction, and introduce you to the Wealth Manifestation Code: a holistic approach to abundance that combines practical strategies with powerful energy clearing techniques.

So, are you ready to unlock your potential for wealth and financial freedom? Let's dive deeper into Chapter 1 and discover the power of the Law of Attraction and the Wealth Manifestation Code!

How the Law of Attraction Can Help You Manifest Wealth

The Law of Attraction works on the principle that everything in the universe is made up of energy. This includes your thoughts, emotions, and actions. When you focus your thoughts and emotions on abundance and success, you create a positive energy that attracts similar energy back to you. This is known as the Law of Attraction in action.

To manifest wealth and abundance, it's important to align your thoughts and emotions with the vibration of wealth. This means focusing on the positive aspects of your financial situation and visualizing your desired outcomes. For example, instead of worrying about debt, focus on the abundance of money that you want to attract into your life.

One way to use the Law of Attraction is to create a **vision board**, also called a dream board. This is a collage of images, words, and phrases that represent your desired outcomes. By looking at your vision board daily, you'll keep your goals and desires at the forefront of your mind, and this will help you attract similar energy towards you.

UPDATE ON THE VISION BOARD METHOD:

One of the readers of this book, who later became my long-term student, told me that although she liked the vision board concept and was familiar with it from the book *The Secret*, she had found a better and more practical alternative: a dream book.

A dream book, or dream list—what some people may also call a bucket list—is essentially the same idea. You write down your dreams, ideally in a three-ring notebook with removable pages, because your dreams will likely change from time to time, and you may need to rewrite them.

The key, just like with the vision board, is to revisit your dream list regularly and, one by one, visualize the positive emotions of how it would feel to live that dream as if you had already achieved it. The goal is to get yourself thinking more often about what you want throughout the day, especially when you are constantly bombarded with negativity and with things that try to pull you down.

As Earl Nightingale said in *The Strangest Secret*, "You become (or you get) what you think about (and feel) most of the time."

I once had another reader approach me and tell me he was using the vision board technique. He had put up an image of himself winning the lottery. However, the problem was that each time he looked at the image, he started to feel doubt because it reminded him of his lack of money and subconsciously threatened his sense of survival.

As the opening quote of this chapter says: "Believe and you shall receive. Doubt and you shall go without."

He did not really believe it. He doubted it.

I asked him why he wanted to win the lottery. He told me that what he really wanted was to be financially free. So I told him to visualize himself being financially free as often as possible. Within about a month, he was approached by a friend who presented him with a lucrative business opportunity that felt right to him.

The key to manifestation is this: Do not obsess over the how. Do not limit the Universe in how it can bring you what you desire. Obsessing over the how only invites doubt and fear, which then bring you more of those same thoughts and feelings. Like attracts like.

As I explain in the next chapter, one of the 33 energy blocks is attachment to a specific outcome, or attachment to the material. You visualize and think about what you want as frequently as possible, and then you release your attachment to it. You maintain that state, and the Universe will present the right how at the perfect time, almost as if by magic. Then you take action—or inspired action, as we will discuss next.

Another key aspect of the Law of Attraction is taking **inspired action** towards your goals. This means taking steps towards your goals that feel natural and enjoyable, rather than forcing yourself to do things you don't enjoy. To effectively engage in this process, begin by identifying your true desires and listening closely to your intuition. This inner guidance often leads to actions that resonate deeply with your personal aspirations.

Stay open to opportunities, even those that appear in unexpected ways, and be prepared to step out of your comfort zone, overcoming any fear and doubt. Remember, the journey towards your goals doesn't have to be monumental steps; starting with small, manageable actions can also create significant impact. These actions should not feel like a chore; instead, they should be activities you look forward to, adding to the joy and richness of your experience.

As you take these steps, maintain a flexible approach, adjusting and reflecting on your actions regularly. If you find certain actions aren't serving your goals or bringing you joy, be willing to change your course. This adaptability ensures that your actions stay aligned with your desires.

When you take inspired action, you create positive momentum that helps you attract more abundance and success. It's about enjoying the process, celebrating small victories, and steadily moving towards your goals in a way that feels fulfilling and right for you.

The Role of Energy Blocks in Wealth Creation

While the Law of Attraction is often touted as a powerful method for wealth manifestation, it involves more than just maintaining positive thoughts. A significant hurdle in this process is the presence of energy blocks. These are essentially limiting beliefs and negative thought patterns that act as barriers, hindering your ability to attract abundance.

Energy blocks can manifest in various forms, such as procrastination, self-doubt, and fear of failure. Often, these issues stem from deeper roots, including past traumas and societal conditioning. For instance, a person who has experienced financial hardship might develop a belief that they are not deserving of wealth. Similarly, societal conditioning can instill limiting beliefs about money and success. For example, one might believe that achieving financial abundance requires excessive hard work or that money is inherently corrupting.

To effectively manifest wealth and abundance, it's crucial to recognize these energy blocks and actively work on clearing them. This process involves introspection and self-awareness, where one must identify and confront these limiting beliefs. By addressing the root causes of these negative thought patterns, whether tied to past experiences or societal influences, one can start to overcome them.

By acknowledging and working through these energy blocks, you can align your thoughts and energies more effectively with your goals. This enhances your ability to use the Law of Attraction for wealth manifestation. Remember, the journey to abundance isn't just about attracting what you desire; it's also about removing the obstacles that prevent those desires from manifesting.

The Wealth Manifestation Code: A Holistic Approach to Abundance

The Wealth Manifestation Code takes a holistic approach to wealth creation by addressing the underlying energy blocks that can hold you back from manifesting abundance. By combining practical strategies with powerful energy clearing techniques, you can clear these blocks and unlock your potential for wealth and financial freedom.

This book will guide you through the process of identifying and clearing the 33 most common energy blocks that can prevent you from manifesting wealth. You'll learn powerful techniques such as meditation, visualization, and energy healing to help you clear these blocks and create a positive energy that attracts abundance into your life.

In the following chapters, we'll dive deeper into each of these energy blocks and explore practical strategies for clearing them. By the end of this book, you'll have a clear understanding of the Wealth Manifestation Code and the tools you need to manifest abundance in all areas of your life. Are you ready to unlock your potential for wealth and financial freedom? Let's dive deeper into the 33 energy blocks and clear your path to abundance!

Chapter 2:
The 33 Energy Blocks to Manifesting Wealth

In this chapter, we'll explore the 33 most common energy blocks that can hinder your ability to manifest wealth. Identifying and clearing these blocks is essential to creating a positive energy that attracts abundance and financial freedom.

Identifying the 33 Energy Blocks that Hinder Wealth Manifestation

The 33 energy blocks to manifesting wealth can be grouped into several categories, including limiting beliefs, negative emotions, and external factors. Some of the most common energy blocks include:

1. I'm not good with money
2. I don't deserve wealth
3. I'll never be able to save enough
4. It's too late to start investing
5. Fear of failure
6. Fear of success
7. Lack of self-worth
8. Negative self-talk
9. Comparing yourself to others
10. Procrastination
11. Inability to finish what you start
12. Lack of focus
13. Lack of motivation
14. Lack of discipline
15. Lack of planning

16. Poor money management skills
17. Overspending
18. Underearning
19. Debt
20. Unhealthy relationship with money
21. Family beliefs and values
22. Cultural conditioning
23. Worrying about the future
24. Negative attachments or feelings towards the past
25. Lack of opportunities
26. Scarcity mindset
27. Attachment to the outcome or material things
28. Unwillingness to accept change
29. Negative influence from others
30. Financial trauma
31. Past failures
32. Lack of trust in the universe
33. Lack of gratitude

If your life right now is not the way you want it to be, chances are that you may be carrying several, or perhaps many, of these energy blocks in your energetic field. Of course, no one has all 33 energy blocks. The highest number I have ever seen is 29 or 30, which is sad, because even from the outside, it was clear that the person's life was deeply burdened.

A common theme running through all of these energy blocks is that each one carries a negative emotion. Emotion is energy in motion, which is why I use the term energy blocks. These blocks are not just ideas in the mind. They are emotional burdens that live within a person and shape the way they think, feel, and move through life. Think of these energy blocks like sandbags tied to a hot-air balloon. If those sandbags are still attached, the balloon cannot rise the way it was meant to. In much the same way, if you are carrying these blocks, you will probably struggle to manifest what you desire until you begin clearing them.

THE WEALTH MANIFESTATION CODE

I am sure that growing up, you saw people around your age in your neighborhood or community who came from wealthy families, or at least from families that were doing quite well financially. You watched them go on vacations, enjoy life more freely, and move through the world with a certain ease. Meanwhile, you and your family may have been struggling just to put food on the table or pay the bills. And even if you did get to go on a vacation from time to time, money may still have been a constant source of stress, worry, or tension in your home.

As the saying goes, some people grow up with a silver spoon in their mouth, while others do not. From my perspective, part of that difference is energetic. Some people grow up without the same level of tightness, heaviness, fear, or emotional burden in their field. As a result, they often develop a more carefree and easygoing relationship with life and money. They seem to attract supportive people, favorable circumstances, and opportunities more naturally, while others struggle to gain the same ground.

One common pattern I often see in people who carry strong energy blocks is debt. Once they begin working and gain access to loans, credit, or borrowed money, they often use it to buy things they believe will somehow fill the void within them— nice clothes, cars, status, or other things they hope will make them feel better. But because their energy field has not been cleared, these things rarely remove the heaviness. In many cases, they only add another layer of burden.

If you are in debt, your main goal should be to free yourself from it so that you can begin clearing your energy field and opening yourself to the life you truly desire. And if your situation feels so difficult that getting out of debt seems impossible, then do not dwell on that thought or the emotions that come with it. By the Law of Attraction, dwelling in those feelings will only attract more of the same. Instead, begin thinking as often as you can from the feeling of financial freedom, as though it were already yours in the present moment. As Earl Nightingale said in The Strangest Secret, "You become (or you get) what you think about (and feel) most of the time."

As you begin clearing even one of these energy blocks, you may find that one or more others begin clearing as well. This is because one block can attract, create, or reinforce others. Like attracts like, and one form of heaviness often strengthens another of a similar kind.

As you continue through this book, the goal is to use the teachings and techniques within it to clear your field of these energy blocks so that you can begin living the life you desire. The difference between you and the person who grew up without money worries may be that they became unconsciously skilled at attracting better experiences because their energy field was clearer, while you may have become unconsciously skilled at attracting struggle because of the heaviness you have carried for so long.

The goal, then, is to become conscious of your patterns, your habits of thought, and your emotional tendencies, and to practice the teachings here until your inner state begins to shift. Over time, you can develop that same ease, that same calmness around life and money, and begin attracting people, events, and circumstances that reflect that new state back to you.

I have been in exactly the situation I am describing, and I have managed to rise out of it and succeed far beyond where I once was. If I can do it, you can do it too. As the saying goes, "As one man can do, you can do also. Believe and you shall receive. Doubt and you shall go without."

Understanding Each Energy Block and Its Effects on Your Finances

Each of these energy blocks can have a significant impact on your ability to manifest wealth. For example, a limiting belief like "I'm not good with money" can create a scarcity mindset that prevents you from taking risks and pursuing opportunities. Negative emotions like fear of failure or success can hold you back from taking action towards your financial goals.

External factors like cultural conditioning, family beliefs and values, and the environment you were raised in can also play a role in shaping your relationship with money. These factors can create limiting beliefs and negative emotions that prevent you from creating abundance in your life.

How to Clear Each Energy Block and Unlock Abundance

The good news is that each of these energy blocks can be cleared with the right techniques and strategies. In the following chapters, we'll explore each energy block in more detail and provide practical tips and tools for clearing them.

Some of the techniques you'll learn include meditation, visualization, affirmations, energy healing, and practical strategies for improving your financial situation. By clearing these energy blocks, you'll create a positive energy that attracts abundance and financial freedom into your life.

In the next chapter, we'll start with the first five energy blocks and explore practical strategies for clearing them. Get ready to unlock your potential for wealth and financial freedom!

Part II:
Clearing Energy Blocks with The Wealth Manifestation Code

Chapter 3:
Clearing Energy Blocks Related to Money Mindset

When it comes to manifesting wealth, your mindset plays a crucial role. The way you think about money, opportunity, risk, and abundance shapes the energy you carry into every decision you make. If your mindset is filled with fear, doubt, hesitation, or hidden resistance, then even when opportunities appear, you may fail to recognize them, trust them, or act on them.

This is why clearing energy blocks related to money mindset is so important. Many people say they want abundance, yet deep within themselves they are still expecting lack, disappointment, or struggle. Their conscious mind may say, "I want more," while their deeper conditioning says, "It is not safe," "It will not last," or "People like me do not get to have that."

In this chapter, we will explore some of the most common energy blocks related to money mindset and how to begin clearing them so that you can create a more open, trusting, and abundant relationship with wealth.

Fear of Scarcity and Lack

One of the most common and powerful energy blocks related to wealth manifestation is the fear of scarcity and lack. This fear can affect the way you think, feel, and act every single day. It can make you overly cautious, hesitant to invest, afraid to take action, and unwilling to trust that more is possible for you.

A person living under the influence of scarcity often feels as though one wrong move will ruin everything. Even when money comes in, they may still feel tense, guarded, or afraid it will disappear. They may struggle to enjoy what they have because their inner state is always preparing for loss. This is how scarcity becomes a vibration: it is not only the lack of money itself, but the constant emotional expectation of lack.

I know this pattern well, because I have experienced it myself.

Many years ago, while I was clearing my own energy blocks and using the manifestation techniques you will learn later in this book, I went through months when the money I had did not seem enough to carry me to the end of the month. In the past, that would have pushed me into the usual patterns of worry, fear, and mental pressure. But instead of giving in to those patterns, I consciously worked to shift my thinking and emotional state in a more positive direction by using the manifestation techniques.

What I often found was that somehow the money would end up being enough, almost as if by magic, or I would unexpectedly receive money in some other way. Sometimes someone would gift me money. Sometimes a small paid opportunity would suddenly appear. Other times, I would sell something that someone happened to need. Most of the time, I ended up with exactly the amount of money I needed to get through the month.

An important detail here is that I did not wake up every day feeling that I needed a miracle to happen, because by the Law of Attraction, I knew that doing so would only produce more of the feeling of needing. Instead, I focused on doing things that helped me feel good, or at least feel better. I chose to trust and believe that things would work out, and most of the time, they did. As the saying goes, "Believe and you shall receive. Doubt and you shall go without."

Now, you may ask: what if your situation is more severe? What if you are already deeply in debt, no one is willing to lend you money because you already owe them, and suddenly an unexpected bill arrives late and is already past due? In that kind of situation, the worst thing you can do is fall into worry, fear, and obsession over how you are going to pay it. Wallowing in worry does not help you. It only reinforces your energy blocks and keeps you in the same heavy state.

What you need to do instead is begin shifting your thinking and emotional state in a more positive direction by using the manifestation methods and techniques you will learn in this book. Even taking a couple of days to calm your system can make a difference. Going for a walk, being close to nature, spending time in a park, listening to birds chirping, or simply looking at trees or distant buildings can also help settle your mind and ease your emotional state.

You may find that as you begin to relax, think better, and feel better, something unexpectedly starts to turn in your favor. A solution may appear, an opening may come, or help may arrive from a direction you did not expect. This has happened to me in the past, and it is one more reason why feeding fear is never the answer. As the saying goes, "Believe and you shall receive. Doubt and you shall go without."

This is why shifting your focus away from lack and toward abundance is such an important part of clearing this particular energy block. Gratitude is one of the strongest ways to do this. Start by appreciating what you do have, even if it seems small. Appreciate your abilities, your opportunities, your relationships, your lessons, and even the simple fact that you are now becoming aware of what must change.

You must also challenge the beliefs that keep scarcity alive. If your mind keeps saying, "There is never enough," "I always fall behind," or "I cannot afford to take a chance," begin replacing those patterns with thoughts that support abundance. For example, you might begin affirming, "There is more available to me than I have allowed myself to see," or "I am open to greater levels of abundance and support."

Scarcity narrows your thinking. Abundance opens it. The more you train yourself to feel and think from abundance, the more your actions begin to change, and the more life begins to reflect that back to you.

Negative Beliefs about Money

Negative beliefs about money are another major energy block that can quietly sabotage wealth manifestation. Many people say they want wealth, but at a deeper level they carry ideas such as "money is corrupt," "rich people are selfish," "wealth changes people for the worse," or "if I become successful, people will resent me."

When these beliefs live in the subconscious mind, they create inner conflict. One part of you may want abundance, while another part fears what abundance means. In that state, you may unconsciously push money away, feel guilty when opportunities arise, or find yourself repeatedly sabotaging your own progress.

To clear this energy block, you need to become honest about what you really believe about money. Ask yourself: What did I hear about money growing up? What did I observe in the people around me? Did I learn that wealth was something noble, useful, and life-giving—or something suspicious, divisive, and dangerous?

Once you identify those beliefs, begin questioning them. Are they actually true? Are they universally true? Or were they simply inherited ideas that you absorbed without ever choosing them consciously?

Then begin replacing them with stronger beliefs that support the life you want to create. For example, instead of "money is bad," you may choose to believe, "Money is a tool that can be used for good." Instead of "wealth corrupts," you may choose, "Wealth in the hands of a good person can bless many lives."

Your beliefs about money matter, because no one fully welcomes what they secretly judge. If you want wealth to come toward you, you must begin making peace with wealth in your own mind.

Resistance to Wealth

Another energy block that often hides beneath the surface is resistance to wealth. This is especially important because many people do not recognize it in themselves. They may say they want more money, more freedom, or more success, yet their actions reveal hesitation, delay, avoidance, and inner tension.

Resistance to wealth does not always look dramatic. Sometimes it looks like procrastination. Sometimes it looks like waiting for the "perfect moment." Sometimes it looks like endlessly planning but rarely moving. Sometimes it looks like shrinking back just when an opportunity appears.

Very often, resistance is rooted in fear. Fear of success. Fear of failure. Fear of responsibility. Fear of being judged. Fear of change. Fear of becoming visible. Fear of losing the familiar version of yourself.

To clear this energy block, you must begin by asking yourself what wealth would truly require from you. What would have to change if more abundance entered your life? What part of you feels threatened by that change? What part of you is still more comfortable with struggle because struggle is familiar?

This is where self-reflection becomes powerful. Sit with the discomfort honestly. Then begin taking action anyway. Not reckless action, but aligned action. Small action. Real action. The kind of action that tells your nervous system, "It is safe for me to move forward."

THE WEALTH MANIFESTATION CODE

The more you take aligned action, the more you weaken the old resistance. Wealth starts to feel less foreign. Success starts to feel less threatening. And abundance begins to feel like something you can truly hold.

In truth, many people are not blocked because wealth is unavailable to them. They are blocked because, at some level, they are still resisting what they claim to want. Once that resistance begins to dissolve, the path becomes far clearer.

In summary, clearing energy blocks related to money mindset is one of the most important parts of the wealth manifestation journey. When you release fear of scarcity, heal negative beliefs about money, and dissolve resistance to wealth, you begin creating a more open inner environment for abundance to enter. And when your inner environment changes, your outer results begin to change as well.

Chapter 4:
Clearing Energy Blocks Related to Self-Worth and Self-Value

In the previous chapter, we focused on clearing energy blocks related to money mindset. In this chapter, we will address energy blocks related to self-worth and self-value, which can significantly affect your ability to manifest wealth.

Many people do not fail to manifest because they lack desire. They fail because, at a deeper level, they do not truly feel worthy of receiving what they are asking for. A person may say they want abundance, success, freedom, or recognition, yet deep within, they may still feel undeserving, unqualified, or not enough.

This inner conflict can quietly sabotage opportunities before they fully take root. That is why clearing energy blocks related to self-worth and self-value is so important.

Self-Doubt and Low Self-Esteem

Self-doubt and low self-esteem are common energy blocks that prevent people from realizing their full potential. When you do not believe in yourself, it becomes much harder to take risks, trust your decisions, or move forward with confidence. Even if opportunities appear, you may hesitate, shrink back, or assume that someone else is more deserving than you are.

To begin clearing this energy block, here are some ways to do that:

1. Use Positive Affirmations

Affirmations are a powerful tool that can help reprogram your subconscious mind. Create affirmations that reflect the qualities you want to embody, such as:

"I am worthy of success and abundance."

"I trust myself to make wise financial decisions."

"I am capable of creating the life I desire."

2. Practice Gratitude for Yourself

Gratitude is not only about being thankful for what is outside of you. It can also be directed inward. Be grateful for your resilience, your growth, your strengths, and the lessons you have survived. This helps shift your identity from lack to value.

3. Celebrate Your Accomplishments

Many people with low self-worth dismiss their own progress too quickly. Take time to acknowledge your achievements, even the small ones. When you celebrate progress, you teach yourself that your effort matters, your growth matters, and you matter.

Inability to Receive

Inability to receive is another major energy block that can interfere with wealth manifestation. Many people are willing to work, strive, sacrifice, and give, yet when something good comes toward them—money, support, recognition, love, or opportunity—they feel uncomfortable receiving it.

This can happen because of guilt, fear, low self-worth, or old conditioning that says receiving is selfish, unsafe, or undeserved. But if you are not open to receiving, then even when life offers you something valuable, you may fail to fully accept it.

To begin clearing this energy block, here are some ways to do that:

1. Practice Receiving in Small Ways

Start by accepting compliments, help, gifts, or support without immediately deflecting them. These small moments train your system to become more comfortable with openness and receiving.

2. Identify Your Money Story

Your money story is made up of the beliefs and emotional associations you hold about money and abundance. For example, if you believe that wealth leads to pressure, judgment, or unhappiness, you may unconsciously resist receiving more. Begin identifying those stories and ask yourself whether they are truly yours—or simply inherited beliefs.

3. Create a Healthier Inner Story

Once you become aware of the old story, begin replacing it with one that supports abundance. For example:

"It is safe for me to receive."

"I can receive abundance with peace and gratitude."

"I do not need to suffer in order to deserve more."

Negative Self-Talk

Negative self-talk is another energy block that can significantly affect your ability to manifest wealth. The voice you carry within yourself shapes your emotions, your expectations, and your decisions. If your inner voice is constantly critical, doubtful, or discouraging, it becomes much harder to move toward abundance with confidence.

Negative self-talk can sound like this:

"I always ruin things."

"I am behind."

"I am not good enough."

"Who do I think I am?"

"People like me do not become successful."

These repeated inner statements create a heavy emotional atmosphere that works against wealth and success.

To begin clearing this energy block, here are some ways to do that:

1. Identify Your Inner Critic

Listen closely to the phrases that repeat in your mind. Notice the statements that pull you into discouragement, hesitation, and self-doubt. You cannot change a voice you refuse to notice.

2. Practice Self-Compassion

Self-compassion means treating yourself with understanding instead of constant attack. When you make mistakes, correct yourself without crushing yourself. This is not weakness. It is emotional maturity.

3. Focus on Your Strengths

Many people are deeply aware of their flaws but disconnected from their strengths. Take time to identify what you do well, what others value in you, and what qualities have helped you endure and grow. The more connected you are to your strengths, the easier it becomes to move through life with confidence and self-respect.

By clearing these energy blocks related to self-worth and self-value, you begin creating a stronger foundation for abundance. When you stop doubting your worth, become more open to receiving, and change the way you speak to yourself internally, you make it easier for wealth, success, and opportunity to enter your life and remain there.

Chapter 5:
Clearing Energy Blocks Related to Relationships and Social Conditioning

Our relationships and social conditioning have a significant impact on our beliefs and attitudes toward money. Many of the blocks people carry around wealth were not created in isolation. They were absorbed from parents, family members, friends, culture, social expectations, and the emotional atmosphere in which they were raised.

Sometimes the blocks you think are yours were handed to you by the people and environment around you.

If you grow up in an environment where money is treated as frightening, shameful, divisive, or always scarce, those associations can quietly settle into your inner world. Without realizing it, you may begin relating to wealth through inherited fear instead of conscious choice.

In this chapter, we will explore the energy blocks related to relationships and social conditioning that may be hindering your ability to manifest wealth and provide strategies for clearing them.

Negative Influences from Family and Friends

Our closest relationships can have a powerful effect on our lives, including our financial well-being. Family and friends shape us not only through what they say, but also through what they repeatedly fear, model, and expect. If the people around you struggled financially, judged wealth negatively, or spoke constantly from worry and limitation, those patterns may have entered your own thinking.

For example, if you grew up hearing stress around bills, debt, or "never having enough," you may have absorbed scarcity long before you were old enough to question it. If successful people were criticized or envied in your home, you may now unconsciously associate wealth with guilt, judgment, or disconnection.

To begin clearing this energy block, here are some ways to do that:

1. Identify What You Inherited

Ask yourself which beliefs about money truly belong to you and which ones were absorbed from family or friends. This step is important because many people are still living from inherited fear without realizing it.

2. Set Healthy Boundaries

You may need to reduce your exposure to people who constantly speak from limitation, negativity, or financial fear. This does not always mean cutting people off. Sometimes it simply means not allowing their emotional state to define your future.

3. Expose Yourself to Better Models

Surround yourself with healthier examples of success, peace, wisdom, and abundance. Learn from people who relate to money in a grounded and constructive way. New examples help weaken old programming.

Unhealthy Relationship with Money

Your relationship with money can also create energy blocks that prevent wealth manifestation. If you relate to money through fear, obsession, guilt, confusion, or emotional neediness, that relationship becomes distorted.

Some people fear money. Some avoid dealing with it. Some overspend to feel better. Some hoard it because they never feel safe. Others chase it desperately, hoping it will fill an emotional emptiness it was never meant to fill. All of these patterns reveal that the relationship itself has become unhealthy.

To begin clearing this energy block, here are some ways to do that:

1. Observe Your Emotional Reactions to Money

Notice how you feel when you think about money. Do you feel peace, or tension? Trust, or fear? Clarity, or confusion? Your emotional reaction often reveals the deeper pattern.

2. Identify Unhealthy Financial Behaviors

Be honest about patterns such as overspending, avoidance, hoarding, guilt, or financial denial. These are not random habits. They often reflect deeper emotional blocks.

3. Build a Healthier Relationship with Money

Begin treating money with more awareness, maturity, and respect. The goal is not to worship money or reject it, but to relate to it more peacefully and intelligently. A healthier relationship with money helps create a healthier energy around it.

Cultural and Social Conditioning

Our broader cultural and social conditioning can also create energy blocks related to wealth manifestation. In many societies, money is either glorified in a shallow way or treated as something shameful, inappropriate, or morally suspicious. Both extremes can create confusion.

Some people were raised in environments where talking openly about money was discouraged. Others absorbed the belief that ambition is selfish, that wanting more is greedy, or that success belongs only to certain kinds of people. These messages can quietly shape the boundaries of what a person believes is possible.

To begin clearing this energy block, here are some ways to do that:

1. Become Aware of Social Messages You Absorbed

Ask yourself what your culture, environment, or social world taught you about wealth, ambition, and success. What did it tell you about people who rise? About people who stand out? About people who want more?

2. Question Those Messages

Not everything you absorbed was true. Some of it was fear. Some of it was limitation disguised as wisdom. Some of it was inherited struggle trying to present itself as realism. Begin challenging the messages that keep you small.

3. Expand Your Inner World

Read books, study successful people, and expose yourself to examples that widen your sense of what is possible. The more your mind expands, the less control old conditioning has over you.

Changing Relationships as Your Energy Changes

One common thing you may notice as you begin clearing energy blocks from your field, using the manifestation techniques, and feeling good more often, is that like-minded individuals may start being drawn to you. Someone may contact you out of the blue, whether you meet by chance in person or connect online through social media or a professional network such as LinkedIn. As you begin talking, you may realize that you share similar thoughts, values, or visions. Trust begins to build, and you may discover that the two of you are a strong match for a business partnership or a joint project. This has happened to me and others multiple times in the past, and I believe it will continue happening because we are manifesting in the right way.

If you are single, you may also find that, when you least expect it, someone special suddenly appears in your life and eventually becomes your long-term partner or spouse. This, too, can be part of the Law of Attraction at work.

On the other hand, you may also notice that certain people begin to grow distant or quietly disappear from your life. This could be an old friend, a family member, or even someone very close to you, such as a sibling, husband, or wife. Sometimes this happens because you and that person are no longer a vibrational match. In a very real sense, as your inner state changes, you begin to change as well. You are no longer the same person you once were, and sometimes that shift affects your ability to remain aligned with certain people.

This is one reason why some relationships, and even some marriages, begin to break apart. It may seem painful or negative at first, but it may actually be the beginning of a new life, or perhaps a better one. Be willing to accept change. If you resist it, you may end up reinforcing another energy block. Remember, one of the 33 energy blocks is unwillingness to accept change.

By clearing energy blocks related to relationships, social conditioning, and vibrational misalignment, you create room for healthier connections, stronger support, and greater abundance to enter your life. Sometimes this means strengthening the right relationships, and sometimes it means outgrowing the wrong ones. Either way, what is truly aligned with you will begin to remain, and what no longer belongs may begin to fall away. Trust that even these changes may be unfolding for your greater good.

"Prayer is not about receiving your manifestation. Prayer is about preparing for your manifestation."

~ The Secret, Rhonda Byrne

Chapter 6:
Applying the Wealth Manifestation Code Techniques

Are you ready to unlock the power of *The Wealth Manifestation Code*? In this chapter, we will explore five powerful techniques that can help you clear your energy blocks and attract abundance into your life. These techniques include meditation and visualization, affirmations and mantras, energy healing and Reiki, journaling and self-reflection, and mindfulness and gratitude practices. Let's dive in!

Meditation and Visualization

Meditation and visualization are powerful tools that can help you tap into the unlimited abundance of the universe. By quieting your mind and focusing on positive thoughts and images, you can create a powerful energy shift that will attract wealth and prosperity into your life. Here's how to get started:

• Find a quiet place where you can sit comfortably and focus on your breath.

• Close your eyes and imagine a bright, white light surrounding you, filling you with positive energy and abundance.

• Visualize yourself living the life of your dreams, with all the wealth, success, and happiness you desire.

• Hold this image in your mind for a few minutes, allowing yourself to feel the joy and excitement of living in abundance.

• When you're ready, slowly open your eyes and carry this positive energy with you throughout your day.

If you find it challenging to visualize images in your mind, especially when it comes to wealth manifestation, don't worry. There are other effective methods to connect with your goals and envision a future abundant in wealth, success, and happiness:

1. **Write About Wealth:** Take a notebook and start jotting down your financial aspirations. Describe your ideal financial situation, the wealth you want to accumulate, and how you plan to use it. Detail your dream investments, luxury items, or charitable acts you'd like to perform. The more you write, the more tangible and achievable these goals become.

2. **Sensory Wealth Visualization:** Focus on the sensory experiences associated with wealth. Imagine the sound of a successful stock market trade, the feel of luxury materials, or the sensation of signing a lucrative deal. Engage your senses to make the experience of wealth more vivid and real.

3. **Emotions of Financial Success:** Concentrate on the feelings that achieving financial success would bring. Picture the joy of financial freedom, the pride in providing for your family, or the satisfaction of reaching your savings goals. Embrace these emotions to fuel your motivation and drive.

Try these out and see which one feels right for you. It's all about finding your own way to connect with the future you want.

One of the readers of an earlier version of this book once contacted me and shared a simple practice that helped him feel better almost immediately. Every day after coming home from work, he would watch beautiful scenes of wealthy islands, such as the Maldives, Bora Bora, or Mauritius, paired with uplifting and upbeat music. He found that this helped him relax, feel lighter, and shift into a better emotional state.

This can be a powerful practice because you are feeding your mind positive imagery while also allowing yourself to feel ease, beauty, and possibility more often. Music by itself can positively affect your emotional state, but when you combine uplifting music with beautiful scenery, the effect can be even stronger because you are engaging both the visual and auditory channels at the same time. If this is something you can do, then do it.

Affirmations and Mantras

Affirmations and mantras are powerful statements that can help you reprogram your subconscious mind and attract abundance into your life. By repeating positive affirmations and mantras daily, you can shift your energy and beliefs about money, success, and prosperity. Affirmations are about impressing the subconscious mind with positive programming to naturally induce a "feel good state," which helps in manifesting your goals, dreams, and desires.

If you have energy blocks, you are probably used—whether subconsciously or consciously, through habit—to using negative affirmations. You may think or say things like, "I don't know if I can do this," "I'm afraid," "But I don't know how," or "I have always…"

It is critical that you become aware of these negative affirmations and begin replacing them with positive and supportive ones such as, "I can do this," "I believe it is possible," "I may not know how right now, but I am certain that the how will present itself in time," "I'm a winner," "I'm willing to do what others don't," and "When the going gets tough, the tough get going. I'm tough."

You can already begin to see how this works. Now, before continuing to the main affirmations in this chapter, there are some essential **power phrases** we need to go through. These phrases can **help activate** *The Wealth Manifestation Code* within you and awaken the true power of affirmations.

Here are the power phrases I advise you to meditate on:

- "What you say, or think, is what you get."
- "The tongue—and the mind—is a creative force."

- "Whether you think you can or whether you think you can't, you're right. It is the thinking that makes it so."
- "You become (or you get) what you think about (and feel) most of the time."
- "Believe and you shall receive. Doubt and you shall go without."
- "Feeling IS the secret."
- "Feel good now."

Here are the essential affirmations and mantras I recommend you use:

- "I am a magnet for wealth and success."
- "I am worthy of abundance and prosperity."
- "Money flows to me easily and effortlessly."
- "I'm so happy and grateful now that money comes to me in increasing quantities on a continuous basis."
- "I am grateful for the abundance in my life."
- "I am the source of my abundance."

Repeat these affirmations and mantras daily, first in the morning and again before bed. You can write them down and place them somewhere visible, such as on your bathroom mirror or computer screen. You can even record them in your own voice, or have someone else record them for you, and listen to them in the morning or at night as you are falling asleep. I have even had readers tell me that they photocopied this page, put it in a frame, and read the affirmations every morning and night, both out loud and silently to themselves. If that works for you, then do it.

While working with my students, I found a variation of this method that worked really well and produced spectacular results. What I asked them to do was to take a blank sheet of lined paper and use a blue ballpoint pen. I specifically asked for blue because it is often associated with activating the emotional side of the mind, which makes the process feel more powerful and engaging.

However, I did not ask them only to write down the affirmations. After writing each one, I asked them to pair it with visualization. For example, if the affirmation was, "I am a magnet for wealth and success," I asked them not only to write it down, but then to pause and picture themselves as if they were literally a physical magnet for wealth and success, and to feel the good emotion of that reality as they visualized it. Then they would repeat the process as many times as possible, either with the same affirmation or a different one.

After just one week, they reported to me that it was as if magic had happened, as though the floodgates of abundance had opened up to them. The effects were truly remarkable. It was a powerful reminder that belief opens the door, while doubt closes it. "Believe and you shall receive. Doubt and you shall go without." And as Earl Nightingale said, "You become (or you get) what you think about (and feel) most of the time."

> Most people give up on affirmations just when they're about to strike gold—it actually takes between 21 to 90 days for them to take full effect. The best practice is to use them during the peaceful times of morning or night when your mind is in a receptive state, open to influence, and ready for positive programming.
>
> Furthermore, it's vital to opt for affirmations that are broad rather than overly specific (like the ones given above). For example, affirmations such as 'I have millions in my bank account' or 'I am a billionaire,' if not reflective of your actual situation, could be more detrimental than beneficial. They might lead to a mental clash because they contradict your present circumstances, prompting your conscious mind to protest, "That's not true!" This internal conflict is akin to waging a war against yourself. Why do that to yourself?
>
> By committing to positive, attainable affirmations, you are more likely to guide your subconscious gently towards realistic goals, thus bypassing any potential for inner conflict.

Simple Ways to Shift Your State

Before moving into deeper energy-healing practices, it is important to understand that shifting your state does not always require a formal technique. Besides meditation, visualization, and affirmations, there are also simple things you can do to help yourself feel better, shift your state, and connect more easily with the reality you desire.

One important thing you must understand is that feeling good, or at least feeling better, is not a small detail in manifestation. It is one of the main keys. If you remain in a heavy, fearful, discouraged, or bitter state for too long, you keep feeding the very energy blocks that are holding you back. That is why learning how to shift your state matters.

Sometimes the shift does not begin with a deep technique. Sometimes it begins with something very simple. Going for a walk. Moving your body. Doing some light exercise. Changing your posture. Smiling, even if only slightly. Listening to uplifting music. Looking at beauty. Sitting in nature. Looking at your vision board or opening your dream book and reconnecting with what you want. If you own something beautiful, such as a really stunning ring or a piece of jewelry you love, you can also put it on and take a moment to admire it. Marveling at beauty, even in a small object, can help shift your state as well. These things may seem small, but they can help interrupt a negative state and begin moving you in a better direction.

You do not always need to go from feeling terrible to feeling amazing. Often, the real goal is simply to feel a little better than you did before. That small shift matters more than most people realize. Once you feel a little better, you think a little better. Once you think a little better, you begin attracting better. This is how the shift begins.

There may also be moments when something suddenly triggers you and pulls you into fear, worry, frustration, or a heavy emotional state. When that happens, it is important to understand that this is often one of your energy blocks being activated. If you immediately give yourself over to that state, it can quickly override your thinking and pull you back into the same old patterns.

In moments like that, do not try to solve your whole life at once. First, interrupt the state. Step away if you need to. Breathe. Go for a walk. Move your body. Change your environment. Stretch. Wash your face. Sit in silence. Pray or listen to prayer. Do whatever helps you begin settling your system and creating even a small amount of relief.

The goal in that moment is not to force yourself to feel amazing. The goal is to stop the emotional spiral before it takes full control. Once the intensity begins to soften, your mind becomes clearer again. And when your mind becomes clearer, you are far less likely to make decisions, speak words, or feed thoughts that strengthen the very energy block that was triggered.

Never underestimate the power of simple actions that help lift your energy. Sometimes one walk, one smile, one stretch, one song, one prayer, or one moment of beauty is enough to begin loosening the grip of a heavy state and opening the door to something better.

Energy Healing and Reiki

Energy healing and Reiki are holistic approaches to wellness, helping you clear energy blocks and balance your chakras for a more abundant life. Here's a concise guide to get started:

1. **Find a Qualified Practitioner or Learn the Techniques**: Look for a skilled Reiki master or energy healer. Many offer training if you wish to practice on yourself.

2. **Set Your Healing Intention:** Before beginning, reflect on your goals, such as physical healing, emotional release, or attracting abundance.

3. **Create a Calm Environment:** Choose a quiet, comfortable space for your session. Consider using soft music or essential oils to enhance relaxation.

4. **Relax and Focus:** Start with deep breathing or meditation to calm your mind. If practicing self-healing, familiarize yourself with basic hand positions, moving gently from your head to your feet, and visualize the energy flowing through your body.

5. **Maintain a Positive Mindset:** During the session, concentrate on positive thoughts and feelings, trusting in the healing process and the universe's support.

6. **Regular Practice and Reflection:** Consistency deepens the benefits. Reflect on your experiences and progress after each session.

By following these steps, whether with a practitioner or through self-practice, you can effectively incorporate energy healing and Reiki into your life for improved well-being and abundance.

Journaling and Self-Reflection

Journaling and self-reflection are powerful tools that can help you uncover your limiting beliefs and negative thought patterns around money and abundance. By taking time to write down your thoughts and feelings, you can gain clarity and create a positive mindset shift. Here's how to get started:

- Set aside time each day to write in your journal, either in the morning or before bed.
- Write down any negative thoughts or beliefs you have about money, success, or prosperity.
- Challenge these beliefs by writing down positive affirmations and mantras.
- Continuously reflect on your journey and take time to celebrate every success, from the significant milestones to the smallest victories. Remember, every step forward, no matter its size, is an essential part of your progress. Each achievement, big or small, matters and contributes to the tapestry of your growth and abundance.

Mindfulness and Gratitude Practices:

Mindfulness and gratitude practices are simple yet powerful ways to increase your vibration, attract abundance, and appreciate the blessings in your life. Here's how to use mindfulness and gratitude practices to manifest wealth:

- Practice mindfulness by taking a few minutes each day to focus on your breath and become aware of your surroundings. Notice the sensations in your body and the sounds around you.
- Express gratitude for the things in your life that you are thankful for. This could be anything from your health, your family and friends, your job, or even the smallest things like a beautiful sunset or a warm cup of tea. Take time to reflect on the positive aspects of your life and focus on the abundance that already exists.

By incorporating these powerful techniques into your daily routine, you can raise your vibration, shift your mindset towards abundance, and manifest the wealth and prosperity that you desire. Remember, the key to manifesting wealth is to focus on the positive aspects of your life, cultivate a sense of gratitude, and believe that abundance is already yours.

Part III:
Integrating The Wealth Manifestation Code into Your Life

Chapter 7:
Building a Wealth Manifestation Mindset

In order to fully integrate the Wealth Manifestation Code into your life, it is essential to develop a positive money mindset, create a wealth manifestation plan, and stay committed to your goals. In this chapter, we'll explore these three key elements in depth and provide practical tips and techniques to help you build a mindset that attracts wealth and abundance.

Developing a Positive Money Mindset

Your mindset is a powerful tool for creating the life you desire, and developing a positive money mindset is essential for attracting wealth and abundance. Here are some tips for cultivating a positive money mindset:

1. **Identify your limiting beliefs**: Take a moment to reflect on your beliefs about money. Are there any limiting beliefs that are holding you back from achieving financial success? Common limiting beliefs include "money is the root of all evil," "rich people are greedy," and "I don't deserve to be wealthy." Once you've identified these limiting beliefs, work on replacing them with positive affirmations and beliefs. For instance, reframe "money is the root of all evil" to "money can be used for good," change "rich people are greedy" to "being wealthy doesn't mean I can't be generous," and turn

"I don't deserve to be wealthy" into "I am worthy of financial success." This shift in mindset is crucial for overcoming barriers to financial prosperity.

2. **Focus on abundance:** Instead of focusing on lack and scarcity, shift your focus to abundance and the opportunities that exist for creating wealth. Practice gratitude for the abundance that already exists in your life, and believe that more abundance is on its way.

3. **Surround yourself with positive influences:** Surround yourself with people who have a positive attitude towards money and success. Seek out mentors and role models who have achieved financial success, and learn from them.

There is also something powerful that happens simply by being in the presence of successful people. When you are around people who carry a higher energy, stronger belief, and a more abundant way of thinking, that influence begins to affect you almost by osmosis. Proximity is powerful. Sometimes, simply being near such people can help you attract better thoughts, better feelings, and, over time, better results.

It can also be very powerful to attend seminars and events where successful or like-minded individuals are present. Being in those environments can expose you to stronger thinking, greater ambition, fresh ideas, and new opportunities. Sometimes one conversation or one connection in the right environment can begin shifting your energy and direction in a powerful way.

If you cannot be around successful people right now for whatever reason, then begin where you can. Listening to the advice of successful people online and hearing their success stories can also begin to shift your vibration. Reading autobiographies and books by successful people can be powerful as well. Of course, it is not exactly the same as being in their direct presence, but it is still a strong start.

Creating a Wealth Manifestation Plan

Once you've developed a positive money mindset, the next step is to create a wealth manifestation plan. This plan will help you clarify your financial goals and take action towards achieving them. Here are some steps to creating a wealth manifestation plan:

1. **Set specific, measurable goals:** Set specific financial goals that are measurable and achievable. For example, you may want to save a certain amount of money, pay off debt, or increase your income.

2. **Create a budget:** Creating a budget is essential for managing your money and achieving your financial goals. Take the time to create a budget that includes all of your income and expenses, and make sure you are living within your means.

3. **Take action:** Once you have your goals and budget in place, it's time to take action. This may involve increasing your income, reducing your expenses, or finding new ways to save money.

Staying Committed to Your Goals

The final key element of building a wealth manifestation mindset is staying committed to your goals. It's easy to get discouraged or distracted along the way, but staying committed to your goals is essential for achieving financial success. Here are some tips for staying committed:

1. **Stay motivated:** Keep your motivation high by reminding yourself of your goals and why they are important to you. Create a vision board or use positive affirmations to stay focused on your vision.

2. **Track your progress:** Keep track of your progress towards your financial goals. This will help you stay motivated and adjust your plan as needed.

3. **Surround yourself with support:** Surround yourself with people who support your financial goals and who will encourage you along the way. Join a community of like-minded individuals or seek out a mentor who can provide guidance and support.

By developing a positive money mindset, creating a wealth manifestation plan, and staying committed to your goals, you can integrate the Wealth Manifestation Code into your life and achieve financial success. Remember that building a wealth manifestation mindset is a journey, and it takes time and effort to create lasting change. But with dedication and persistence, you can transform your relationship with money and attract abundance into your life.

Chapter 8:
Taking Action with the Wealth Manifestation Code

Now that you have developed a wealth manifestation plan and a positive money mindset, it is time to take action towards your financial goals. Here are some practical steps to help you align your actions with your wealth manifestation plan, build a support system for wealth creation, and overcome obstacles and challenges:

1. **Aligning Your Actions with Your Wealth Manifestation Plan:** Your wealth manifestation plan outlines your financial goals and the steps you need to take to achieve them. To align your actions with your plan, you need to break down your goals into smaller, actionable steps. For example, if your goal is to save $10,000 in a year, you can break it down into saving $834 each month or $208 each week. Once you have a clear idea of what you need to do, make a schedule and stick to it. Hold yourself accountable for your actions and track your progress regularly.

2. **Building a Support System for Wealth Creation:** Building a support system is crucial for staying motivated and accountable. Surround yourself with people who share your financial goals, values, and desire for growth. Join a community of like-minded individuals or work with a financial coach to help you stay on track. You can also find an accountability partner who helps you remain committed to your goals. Share your progress and successes with your support system, and celebrate each milestone you achieve.

3. **Overcoming Obstacles and Challenges:** No matter how well-planned your wealth manifestation journey is, there will be obstacles and challenges along

the way. It is essential to develop resilience and a growth mindset to overcome these obstacles. When facing a challenge, ask yourself what you can learn from it and how you can use it to grow. Seek help from your support system or a financial expert if needed. Remember that setbacks are part of the journey, and each one provides an opportunity for growth.

Ultimately, taking action is the most crucial step in the wealth manifestation process. Aligning your actions with your plan, building a support system, and developing resilience will help you overcome obstacles and achieve your financial goals. Remember to celebrate each milestone and share your progress with your support system. With the Wealth Manifestation Code and a positive mindset, you can manifest the wealth and abundance you desire.

Conclusion

As you conclude your journey through The Wealth Manifestation Code, it's essential to recognize the power this system has in unlocking abundance and prosperity in your life. By identifying and clearing the 33 energy blocks that may be holding you back from achieving your goals, you open yourself up to a world of possibilities and opportunities.

With the Wealth Manifestation Code, you can take control of your financial destiny and live a life filled with abundance and fulfillment. By feeling better, developing a positive money mindset, creating a wealth manifestation plan, and staying committed to your goals, you can begin manifesting your desires into reality and attracting wealth and success into your life.

However, this journey is not always easy. It requires you to align your actions with your wealth manifestation plan, build a support system for wealth creation, and overcome obstacles and challenges that may arise along the way. But with determination, perseverance, and the right mindset, you can overcome any obstacle and achieve the abundance you desire.

As I release this latest edition of the book, there are global external events taking place that, for many people, may be a source of fear, worry, and even panic. If you find that your state has shifted because of something happening outside of you, I want to encourage you to take back control and use the techniques in this book to help guide yourself back to the state you desire—to feeling better, thinking more clearly, and returning to the right track.

I am not asking you to deny the reality of your situation. Your circumstances may be real, and depending on where you are, you may be affected adversely, even severely. If that is the case, then my heart goes out to you. But even then, I want you to remember this: you still have the power to begin taking back control of your thoughts, your feelings, and, depending on the circumstances, some of your actions.

I once had a mentor tell me about a friend of his who was asked by financial analysts how his businesses were doing so well at a time when the country was going through one of its greatest recessions. His reply was, "I may know that the country is in a recession, but I choose not to participate." In other words, he directed his thoughts and feelings toward what he wanted rather than toward what he did not want, and in doing so, he manifested a different reality.

Remember: "As one man can do, you can do also. Believe and you shall receive. Doubt and you shall go without."

If you have made it this far, it means you are serious about changing your financial and personal life for the better. That already sets you apart. Many people want a better life, but not everyone is willing to do the inner work that real change requires.

Keep reading, because there is still additional information in the pages that follow that may help you even further. And do not read this book only once. Return to it again and again. Each rereading can deepen the message, reinforce the right patterns, and help you continue clearing the energy blocks that may still be working beneath the surface.

Ultimately, *The Wealth Manifestation Code* is a powerful tool that can help you unlock your full potential and live the life of your dreams. By implementing the techniques and practices outlined in this system, you can tap into the unlimited abundance of the universe and manifest your desires into reality. So go forth with confidence, trust in the power of *The Wealth Manifestation Code*, and watch as your life transforms into one of abundance and fulfillment.

The Power Phrases

Here are the power phrases we used throughout this book to **help activate** *The Wealth Manifestation Code*. I intentionally say help activate, because these phrases are not, by themselves, what activate *The Wealth Manifestation Code*. What truly activates it are the various methods and techniques taught throughout this book.

Think of the main techniques as the soil, and the power phrases as the fertilizer that helps produce the best and most desired fruit. In other words, these phrases help strengthen, reinforce, and deepen the work you are already doing.

Here are the power phrases:

- "What you say, or think, is what you get."
- "The tongue—and the mind—is a creative force."
- "You become (or you get) what you think about (and feel) most of the time."
- "As one man can do, you can do also."
- "Whether you think you can or whether you think you can't, you're right. It is the thinking that makes it so."
- "Believe and you shall receive. Doubt and you shall go without."
- "Like attracts like, or that which is similar."
- "Feeling IS the secret."
- "Feel good now."

Special Bonus!

Here's a special treat for the readers who made it to the very end of this book. Remember those powerful affirmations from Chapter 6? I've now brought them to life, narrated in both male and female voices. But there's a twist – they are intertwined with magical solfeggio frequencies and root chakra tones to supercharge their impact. Why this particular combination? Solfeggio frequencies, ancient keys to healing and transformation, elevate affirmations from mere words to a vibrational healing experience, unlocking various aspects of your well-being.

The inclusion of root chakra frequencies adds a grounding force, connecting you to a sense of security and belonging. Known as the "money chakra," a balanced root chakra is crucial for manifesting abundance and financial stability. This creates the perfect foundation for your affirmations to take root and flourish. This blend of sound waves doesn't just reach your ears; it resonates with your very cells, enhancing the affirmations' power to manifest positive changes in your life. It's akin to giving your journey of growth and self-discovery a powerful boost.

Here are the links for the audio tracks:

Male Voice Audio: https://bit.ly/male-affirmations

Female Voice Audio: http://bit.ly/female-affirmations

It's worth noting that certain parts of the audio, or the nuances in the voices, might not be immediately soothing or easy on the ears. However, I urge you to persist with them for 21 days to effectively rewire your subconscious mind. This period is crucial for acclimation and for achieving the full benefits of the affirmations. Feel free to adjust the volume to a comfortable level, though I generally recommend keeping it low, as this may be better for allowing the affirmations to sink into the subconscious. If the audio doesn't resonate with you, consider crafting your own recording. Doing so might extend the time it takes to see their effects, often up to 90 days, but it is a deeply personal way to integrate these powerful affirmations into your life. This approach offers another profound avenue for embedding these affirmations into the fabric of your existence.

Frequently Asked Questions

1. What are the correct categories for the 33 energy blocks mentioned in the Wealth Manifestation Code?

Answer: *The Wealth Manifestation Code* categorizes the 33 energy blocks into these three main groups:

1. **Limiting Beliefs:** These are negative thought patterns that can restrict your mindset and prevent you from achieving financial success.

2. **Negative Emotions:** Emotions like fear, guilt, or shame that hold you back from pursuing wealth and taking financial risks.

3. **External Factors:** Conditions beyond your control, such as cultural norms or family beliefs, that can shape your attitude toward money and wealth.

2. Can you divide the 33 blocks into these categories to help me understand them better?

Answer: Sure! Here's how the 33 energy blocks can be divided into the correct categories:

Limiting Beliefs:

- I'm not good with money
- I don't deserve wealth
- I'll never be able to save enough
- It's too late to start investing
- Lack of self-worth
- Scarcity mindset
- Lack of trust in the universe

Negative Emotions:

- Fear of failure
- Fear of success
- Negative self-talk
- Comparing yourself to others
- Procrastination
- Inability to finish what you start
- Lack of focus
- Lack of motivation
- Lack of discipline
- Worrying about the future
- Negative attachments or feelings towards the past
- Attachment to the outcome or material things
- Unwillingness to accept change
- Financial trauma
- Past failures
- Lack of gratitude

External Factors:

- Lack of planning (in some cases, this can also be due to negative emotions)
- Poor money management skills
- Overspending
- Underearning
- Debt
- Unhealthy relationship with money

- Family beliefs and values
- Cultural conditioning
- Lack of opportunities
- Negative influence from others

3. How do I find the right technique for each block, and do I have to use all the techniques on each one, one by one?

Answer: To find the best technique for each block, focus on its root cause. Here's a general guide:

1. **For Limiting Beliefs:** Techniques like affirmations, positive self-talk, and visualization help reframe your mindset.

2. **For Negative Emotions:** Meditation, journaling, gratitude, visualization, breathwork, and emotional awareness can help you process and release these emotional blocks.

3. **For External Factors:** Practical action is often needed here. This may include building better financial habits, creating a plan, setting boundaries, becoming more aware of inherited patterns, and making conscious changes in the way you relate to money and your environment.

You do not have to use every technique on every block. Start by identifying the blocks that are strongest in your life, and then choose the techniques that resonate with you most. The key is to be consistent.

Although I have given you general guidance on which techniques may work best for energy blocks in each of the three categories, do not miss the deeper point. The main goal is awareness, not technique. Your task is to become aware of which energy block is active, how it is trying to pull you back into old patterns of thinking, feeling, and acting, and then work on it consciously—resolving it, correcting it, and directing yourself toward a new and more desired way of being.

Also remember that when you begin clearing one energy block, you may find that one or more others start clearing as well. This is because one block can attract, create, or reinforce others. Like attracts like, and one form of heaviness often strengthens another of a similar kind.

4. How do I know exactly which energy block or blocks are holding me back?

Answer: To identify which energy blocks are holding you back, engage in deep meditation and self-reflection. Through this practice, you can gain insights into the obstacles affecting your progress. For example, if you discover that <u>procrastination</u> and <u>an inability to finish what you start</u> are significant blocks for you, delve deeper to uncover the underlying cause. You might find that these behaviors stem from self-worth or self-esteem issues, where you struggle to believe in the value of your work or the contribution you can make to the world. This process of introspection can help you pinpoint the root of your energy blocks, enabling you to address them more effectively.

If you're having difficulty clearing your mind due to stress or a personal crisis, consider spending time in nature. Being in a natural setting can calm your mind, enhance your clarity of thought, and boost your creativity. This connection with nature can provide the mental space needed to gain deeper insights and make more effective progress in identifying and overcoming your energy blocks.

5. Why are almost all the techniques in the book mental and don't work on the physical?

Answer: This book delves into the fascinating connection between our inner world and external reality. It emphasizes the profound impact of our thoughts, beliefs, and emotions on manifesting wealth. By honing our mindset, aligning our energy, and exploring the depths of our subconscious, we unlock the keys to abundance. As we transform ourselves from within, our external circumstances naturally align with our newfound wealth consciousness. The purpose of this book is to shed light on the unconscious patterns and limitations holding us back, enabling us to consciously resolve and release them. By making the unseen seen, we empower ourselves to manifest wealth and abundance with clarity and intention.

6. How can I effectively implement the teachings in this book and ensure lasting results, especially if I struggle with staying committed and tend to revert to old habits?

Answer: Implementing lasting change requires a practical and incremental approach. Drawing inspiration from the Japanese method of Kaizen, focus on taking small, manageable steps towards your goals. Break down the teachings in this book into smaller, actionable tasks that you can consistently incorporate into your daily routine. Start with one simple habit and commit to practicing it consistently for a specific period. As you build momentum and experience success, gradually add new habits and expand your practice. By embracing the philosophy of continuous improvement and celebrating small victories, you can overcome resistance to change and create a sustainable transformation in your life.

Remember, consistency is key. Even if progress feels slow at times, trust in the power of small, consistent actions to create lasting change. Stay committed to your growth journey, seek support from like-minded individuals or a mentor, and celebrate every step forward, no matter how small. With patience, perseverance, and a Kaizen mindset, you can successfully implement the teachings in this book and break free from old habits to manifest abundance in your life.

7. How long does it take to see results using the Wealth Manifestation Code?

Answer: The timeline for seeing results varies for each individual. It depends on various factors such as the depth of your energy blocks, your commitment to the techniques, and the level of belief and alignment you achieve. Some may experience significant shifts in a short period, while for others, it may take more time. Trust the process, stay consistent, and have faith in the unfolding of your abundance journey.

8. How do I know that I have cleared my energy blocks?

Answer: You'll know you've cleared your energy blocks when you start noticing positive changes in your thoughts, emotions, and actions. Here are some signs to look for:

1. **Increased Confidence and Self-Worth**: You feel more self-assured, believing in your work, abilities, and decisions.
2. **Improved Emotional Well-being**: You experience a greater sense of peace, happiness, and emotional balance.
3. **Enhanced Motivation:** You find it easier to stay focused, motivated, and driven towards your goals.
4. **Better Financial Habits:** You develop healthier financial behaviors, such as saving more, spending wisely, and investing confidently.
5. **Positive Relationships:** Your interactions with others improve, and you attract supportive and uplifting relationships.
6. **Greater Abundance:** You notice an increase in opportunities, resources, and overall abundance in your life.
7. **Inner Alignment:** You feel more aligned with your values, passions, and purpose, leading to a sense of fulfillment and joy.

Remember, clearing energy blocks is a continuous process. Regularly practicing the techniques in the book and staying mindful of your thoughts and emotions will help you maintain a clear and positive energy flow, allowing you to manifest wealth and abundance more effectively.

9. How do I handle setbacks or challenges that arise during my wealth manifestation journey?

Answer: Setbacks and challenges are a natural part of any transformative process. When faced with obstacles, remember to maintain a positive mindset and view challenges as opportunities for growth and learning. Utilize the techniques in the book to shift your energy, reframe limiting beliefs, and find creative solutions. Seek support from mentors, coaches, or like-minded individuals who can provide guidance and encouragement during challenging times.

Remember, each person's journey is unique, and it's important to trust your own inner guidance as you navigate the wealth manifestation process. Embrace the teachings, stay committed to your growth, and watch as your abundance and wealth unfold.

10. Why do bad people sometimes seem lucky or end up rich?

Answer: The Law of Attraction does not care whether a person is morally good or bad. It works as a law. It responds to what a person consistently thinks, feels, and radiates.

Someone may be a bad person in character, yet still be internally focused, confident, and emotionally aligned with the outcomes they want. If they are not heavily burdened by doubt, fear, or other energy blocks in that area of life, they may still attract success, money, or favorable results much of the time.

This does not mean they are truly at peace, spiritually mature, or free from consequences. It simply means that the Law of Attraction responds to vibration, alignment, and dominant inner state. Like attracts like.

11. Can I use sound therapy or TFT along with the techniques and methods from the Wealth Manifestation Code?

Answer: Yes, you can! Sound therapy and Thought Field Therapy (TFT) are great additions to the tools and techniques outlined in the Wealth Manifestation Code.

Sound therapy uses calming sounds and vibrations to help you relax. Instruments like singing bowls, tuning forks, or gongs create soothing vibrations that can reduce stress and improve your mood. This positive energy can support your journey toward manifesting wealth.

Thought Field Therapy (TFT), created by psychologist Roger Callahan, is a tapping technique. By tapping specific points on your body in a particular sequence, TFT aims to restore balance to your energy system, helping to release emotional stress and negative thoughts.

TFT may be especially helpful if you are going through something severe, such as trauma, a breakup, or deep emotional distress, and find that no matter what you do, you cannot seem to shift yourself into a better state through conscious effort alone. However, a word of caution: TFT is best practiced under the guidance of a qualified professional. In most cases, it is difficult to apply it correctly and achieve meaningful results simply by watching instructional videos online.

TFT might take some practice since it's more complex, but it can be very effective for those who resonate with it. Sound therapy, on the other hand, is generally more accessible and easier to try.

Both sound therapy and TFT can help you clear energy blocks. If you're interested in exploring them, consider working with experienced practitioners to guide you. These techniques can offer unique ways to create a positive energy that aligns with your wealth goals.

Help This Book Reach Others

If this book has truly helped you, then I would kindly ask you to leave a review on Amazon or Goodreads.

Your review is not a small thing. It can help this book reach someone who is still trapped in the very patterns, burdens, and blocks this message was written to help break. Sometimes one honest review is all it takes for a person to say, "This is the book I need right now."

If *The Wealth Manifestation Code* has helped you think differently, feel differently, begin freeing yourself from what has been holding you back, and become more open to the possibility of abundance, then kindly share that. Your words may do far more than you realize.

Thank you for reading, and thank you for helping this book reach others.

Yours truly,

Simon Bedros

Ready for the Next Step?

If you've made it this far, you've already done powerful inner work—clearing the 33 energy blocks that were holding you back from manifesting wealth and freedom. But here's something I've discovered through working with thousands of people on their transformation journey:

Even after clearing the blocks... some people still feel stuck.

Why?

Because there's one final layer that most overlook—**the need to control.**

You may still be holding on to outcomes. To expectations. To past pain. To tension in your body, your mind, and your energy field. This hidden grip—this *energetic tightness*—can quietly undo all the work you've done. That's where surrender comes in.

Surrender isn't weakness. It's the missing link.

In my follow-up book, *The Art of Surrender,* I go deeper. I explore how to release control, let go of the emotional baggage, and shift your energy into a state of *allowing*. Because when you're no longer pushing or forcing, you align with the natural flow of abundance, love, and peace.

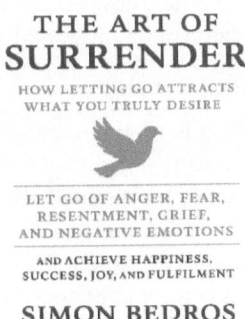

If *The Wealth Manifestation Code* cleared your path... Then *The Art of Surrender* shows you how to *walk it with grace*.

Let go. And finally receive.
That's the next phase of your journey.

Get your copy of *The Art of Surrender* today.

Go to Amazon and search:
The Art of Surrender by Simon Bedros

Or simply scan the QR code below to go directly to the book:

And once you begin clearing what is blocking you, surrendering what no longer serves you, and manifesting more of what you truly want, there comes another important stage. Once the Universe gives you the right how, the next question becomes: how do you make the most of it? How do you turn opportunity into real momentum, meaningful progress, and lasting success?

That is where my other book, *THE SUCCESS CREATION FORMULA: A Proven System for Turning Your Dreams into Reality – The Missing Secrets Revealed*, comes in. While *The Wealth Manifestation Code* helps you clear the path, and *The Art of Surrender* helps you release control and walk that path with more grace, *The Success Creation Formula* helps you maximize your effort, sharpen your direction, and create stronger results.

In that book, I introduce a three-part framework for creating successful outcomes and building real success more consistently. It is designed to help you get the maximum from your efforts, use your energy more wisely, and turn the opportunities you have manifested into tangible progress and meaningful achievement.

Get your copy of *THE SUCCESS CREATION FORMULA: A Proven System for Turning Your Dreams into Reality – The Missing Secrets Revealed* today.

Go to Amazon and search:

The Success Creation Formula by Simon Bedros

Or simply scan the QR code to go directly to the book.

And there is one more book of mine that may speak to you deeply, especially if you sense that some of the weight you carry goes beyond wealth, success, or manifestation itself.

CLEARING THE SAMSKARAS: HOW TO FREE YOURSELF FROM THE PAST is about something slightly different, though closely related. While *The Wealth Manifestation Code* focuses on identifying and clearing the energy blocks that may be interfering with abundance and wealth manifestation, Clearing the Samskaras goes deeper into the unseen impressions left by your past.

THE WEALTH MANIFESTATION CODE

Every moment leaves a trace.

Every thought, emotion, and action impresses itself into the subtle fabric of your mind and body. These impressions—known in the yogic tradition as samskaras—shape how you see yourself, how you react, what you carry, and how you move through life.

This book is less about manifestation itself and more about learning how to live an unburdened life. It is about understanding the hidden imprints of the past, meeting them with awareness and compassion, and gradually freeing yourself from the conditioning that has been weighing on you for far too long.

There are similarities between the two books, because both deal with unseen inner patterns that shape outer experience. But *The Wealth Manifestation Code* is more focused on clearing the blocks that interfere with wealth, abundance, and manifestation, while *Clearing the Samskaras* is more focused on helping you release the deeper impressions of the past so you can live with more clarity, peace, and inner freedom.

You may want to get this book if you feel that no matter how much you try to move forward, something old still seems to pull you back—an emotional weight, a recurring inner pattern, or a past wound that has not fully released. If that speaks to you, then this book may help you understand what you are carrying and how to begin freeing yourself from it.

Get your copy of *CLEARING THE SAMSKARAS: HOW TO FREE YOURSELF FROM THE PAST* today.

Go to Amazon and search:

Clearing the Samskaras by Simon Bedros

Or simply scan the QR code to go directly to the book.

About the Author

Simon Bedros is a successful entrepreneur, bestselling author, strategic advisor, and visionary mentor. His mission is to empower ambitious individuals to rise above self-imposed limits, unlock their highest potential, and create lives of extraordinary success and lasting purpose.

After successfully exiting his startup business, Bedros devoted himself fully to writing transformative books and mentoring those ready to realize their potential. His work has helped countless individuals turn adversity into strength and live with greater clarity, intention, and direction.

Before launching his consulting career, he spent nearly a decade in high-impact roles with industry leaders, where he discovered his passion for transformation and leadership.

Over the years, Bedros has guided thousands of businesses — from mid-size enterprises to global leaders such as Google, Visa, Salesforce, Oracle, and MetLife — toward remarkable growth. His guidance in sales, marketing, and crisis management has impacted organizations worldwide, reflecting his ability to navigate complexity and drive transformation at every level.

His influence extends beyond his books. Through writing, mentoring, and daily reflections shared online, he continues to inspire thousands to cut through the noise, embrace clarity, and take bold steps toward the lives they truly desire.

In every endeavor — whether writing, mentoring, or speaking — Bedros remains committed to awakening vision, empowering disciplined action, and guiding individuals toward lives of clarity, impact, and meaningful achievement.

To explore one-on-one mentoring with Simon or learn more about his inner circle program, connect with him on LinkedIn or through one of his social media channels.

www.ingramcontent.com/pod-product-compliance
Lightning Source LLC
Chambersburg PA
CBHW031539210526
45464CB00003B/1070